hope
re

First published in the UK in 2011 by The Salariya Book Company Ltd
This edition published in the UK in 2024 by Hatch Press,
an imprint of Bonnier Books UK
4th Floor, Victoria House
Bloomsbury Square, London WC1B 4DA
Owned by Bonnier Books
Sveavägen 56, Stockholm, Sweden
www.bonnierbooks.co.uk

1 3 5 7 9 10 8 6 4 2

ISBN 978-1-80078-892-3

Printed in the United Kingdom

You Wouldn't Want to...

BE IN THE
ANCIENT GREEK OLYMPICS

Written by David Stewart
Illustrated by David Antram

Hatch

Contents

Introduction

It is the middle of the fifth century BC and you are a young boy living in a small farming village outside Athens in Greece. You are growing up during the height of the Greek civilisation. Twenty years ago, Greece successfully fought off an invasion by the Persians. In the mood of optimism that has followed, theatre, poetry, music and architecture are all flourishing. Under the rule of the brilliant politician, Pericles, Athens has established a democracy, meaning that every citizen can have his say in the way the city-state is run.

Your father, who fought in the Persian Wars, is a strict man with great ambitions for his family. He has saved all his money so that you can attend school and learn the arts, music and above all, athletics. He wants you to bring honour and respect to your family name by competing in the greatest contest of all – the Olympic Games, first held in 776 BC. The training will be hard and the competition fierce. For a young boy who prefers the easy life, the last thing you want to do is enter the Olympics!

It's a man's world

Your father, like many of the villagers outside Athens, works hard on his farm. He wants a better life for his son.

Fifth-century Greece is divided into city-states. Athens is the largest and a centre of commerce, culture and learning. On a hill, the Acropolis houses the magnificent official buildings of the city, including the Parthenon. Like most Greek city-states, people are not treated equally. They are divided into those who are allowed to vote, called citizens, and those who are not, often women, slaves or foreigners. Most people are poor, and only boys from wealthy families receive a proper education. Your father makes you get up early every day to walk to school in the city.

Your mother and sister are under your father's complete control. Your sister cannot attend school and will never have the same rights as you. Your father chooses whom your sister marries.

Pericles

PERICLES

A great leader and statesman came to power in 461 BC and introduced the concept of democracy (meaning 'rule by the people'). This means that all male citizens of Athens can meet and vote in Athenian politics.

Handy hint

Don't grow up! After the age of six, your mother stops looking after you. You have to give up your toys and your father takes charge of you.

Training – no pain, no gain!

Your schoolteachers are strict, but you enjoy your lessons and work hard. The main part of your education revolves around Greece's history, which includes learning vast amounts of philosophy and poetry by heart. When you reach your teens, physical education becomes just as important as your other lessons.

The Greeks believe that people should strive for excellence in all areas and must exercise their bodies as well as their minds. You are trained in sports such as wrestling, running, javelin, discus and long jump which all take place in the *palaestra*, a sports ground attached to the school.

Subjects at school

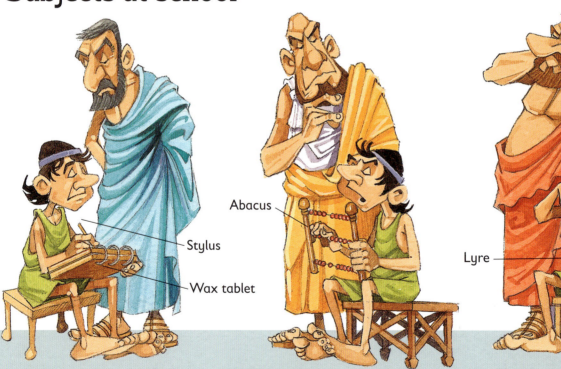

Stylus

Wax tablet

Abacus

Lyre

WRITING
Writing is an important part of your education. Instead of writing on paper, you are taught to inscribe letters on wax tablets with a stylus. This means you can easily smooth over mistakes.

MATHEMATICS
Though not as important as literature, you are taught arithmetic by counting beads on an abacus. If you ever take a job as an official in the city, this will be a very significant skill.

MUSIC
The Greeks believe that playing music can make you a better person. You practise hard on a stringed instrument called a lyre, which is often used to accompany poetry recitals.

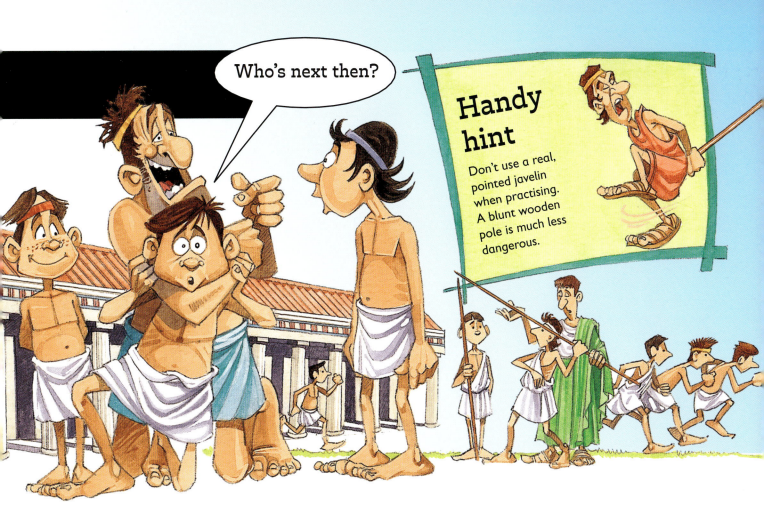

Handy hint

Don't use a real, pointed javelin when practising. A blunt wooden pole is much less dangerous.

THE HARDSHIPS OF WAR

Physical education is also admired because it will prepare you should the city-state ever go to war. Your father had to fight the Persians between 490 and 480 BC and thinks you need some toughening up.

9

Military service

At the age of 18, you become an *ephebe*. This means you are ready to become a citizen, but first you must prove yourself worthy. *Ephebes* must live by strict rules for two years, including a period of compulsory military service. Learning to be a soldier is tough, but your physical training is going well and you become the strongest young man in your school.

Instead of joining the army, your father wants you to prove yourself in an athletic competition. There are several of these in ancient Greece but the most famous is the Olympic Games. The Games occur every four years (a period called an olympiad) and attract athletes from all over the land.

ITALY

MILITARY TRAINING
All the athletics you took part in at school comes in handy now. You have to go on long marches and learn to throw real spears.

Map showing ancient Greece and some of its city-states

GREECE
Aegean Sea
Athens
Olympia
Sparta
Mediterranean Sea

Handy hint

Take a sun-shade on your journey – the weather gets very hot and when it rains you'll have an umbrella.

You call yourselves real men?!

TO COMPETE

You must travel across Greece as a pilgrim to the sanctuary at Olympia. It's a long way and you must make the journey on foot. Don't worry about passing through hostile lands – it is forbidden to attack a pilgrim during the Olympic truce.

When you arrive at Olympia, the place is a bustle of activity. Male athletes from all over the Greek world have come to take part – women are not allowed to enter. You are astounded at how beautiful the place is. Temples and other marble buildings rise amongst the olive and cypress trees. The Games will not start for another ten months, so you have plenty of time for training and you will eat, exercise and sleep with the other athletes. Above all, the Games are a religious festival, sacred to the god Zeus. To ensure the gods look favourably upon you, you visit the Temple of Zeus regularly to make offerings.

(1) Temple of Zeus; (2) training ground; (3) stadium; (4) hippodrome (for equestrian races); (5) treasuries; (6) Temple of Hera (Zeus's wife)

ZEUS is the king of the Greek gods and is believed to carry a thunderbolt to hurl at his enemies. The whole sanctuary at Olympia is sacred to him and the largest temple houses his enormous statue made from ivory and gold.

Zeus

UPON YOUR ARRIVAL

At the sanctuary of Olympia, you must register your participation in the upcoming competition. Officials check that you are a Greek by birth and not a foreigner or slave. Non-Greeks are not allowed to take part in the sacred Games.

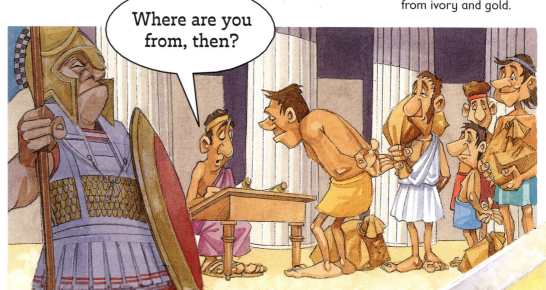

Where are you from, then?

SACRIFICES

These vary depending on how wealthy you are. The very rich might set up their own shrines and sacrifice whole herds of cattle, but you could sacrifice sheep, goats, poultry, or just make offerings of wine or a few grains of wheat.

THE FINISHED ARTICLE

After ten months of sacrifices and healthy living, you are at the peak of your physical prowess and are eager for the Games to begin.

13

Time to compete

Finally the summer arrives and the Games begin. They will last for five days. On the first you must take the oath of *aidos*, or sportsmanship. You are afraid of under-performing in front of so many people, especially your father. He wants you to bring honour to your family and home by winning. Spectators, both rich and poor, have travelled to watch the events. Most people sleep outdoors at night, which is no problem in the hot Greek summer. Among the crowds, there are gamblers and salesmen, all trying to make money from the competition.

What is the meaning of life?

Philosopher

Watch out for:

Pickpockets

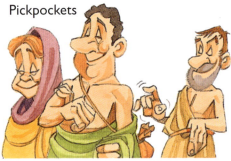

PICKPOCKETS
Though the competition is a religious event, not all the spectators are honourable. The large crowds at Olympia attract all sorts of undesirable characters.

POETS AND PHILOSOPHERS
Philosophy (meaning 'love of wisdom') is a popular pastime in ancient Greece. Learned men come to the Olympics to discuss ideas and to write poems.

ACTORS
Greeks love a good play, especially tragedies. The actors wear masks with exaggerated expressions to help show how their characters feel.

DOCTORS
If you become injured, doctors will be near at hand to help you. However, most don't know what they are doing.

Doctor

Actors

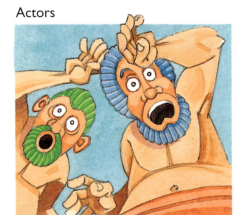

Javelin

THE PENTATHLON

You will be taking part in a competition called the pentathlon. It is made up of five different disciplines and requires all-round physical strength. The five separate events are: javelin, long jump, discus throwing, running and wrestling. Though you have practised all of them since you were a boy, now you will be put to the ultimate test.

Handy hint

After last-minute practising, go down to the river to bathe and purify yourself. It's cold, but it will be worth it.

Long jump

Halteres (weights)

Discus

Running

Wrestling

At the stadium

Up to 50,000 spectators gather on the slopes around the stadium. The oldest and most important event at the Games is running. The noise from the crowd is deafening but you must concentrate on the race ahead. An announcer reads out your name and place of birth. You take off your clothes in a small building at the side of the stadium and rub yourself down with olive oil. Everyone competes in the nude as a symbol of purity. There's no need to be embarrassed – women are not allowed to watch the competitions.

Though your race is run in the nude, there is another race in which the runners have to wear helmets and carry shields. The race is called the *hoplitodromos*, because Greek soldiers are called 'hoplites'.

RUNNING
You must run one length of the stadium, which is nearly 200 metres long. The race is run barefoot across the sand. It is hard going and you have to be careful not to collide with the other contestants.

THE FIRST MARATHON

In 490 BC, during the Persian Wars, a messenger ran all the way – 42km – from the plains of Marathon to Athens to announce an Athenian victory. Though there were no long races in the original Games, this event inspired the marathon in the modern Olympics.

I'm sure that was a false start!

A false start will mean disqualification, so make sure you don't set off before the trumpet sounds. Other running events include completing two and six lengths of the track.

Starting blocks

Practice makes perfect

Athletes at the Games are fine physical specimens, men who have been in training for months. Your technique will have to be spot on if you are going to win. Warm up well and rub oil into your body to make yourself limber. Other athletes pose for the crowd, flexing their muscles, but you must focus. Don't think about them, or your father, watching from the stands. Musicians (flautists) play to help you relax and to entertain the crowd.

The discus event involves throwing three heavy, polished clay disks as far as possible. You throw from a raised mound and will need a strong arm. You are very good at the javelin because your military training involved throwing a spear.

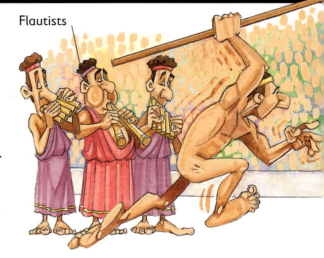

Flautists

RIGHT ON TARGET

There are two elements to being good at the javelin. You must be able to throw a long way, but also accurately.

The long jump does not have a run up. Distance is achieved by carrying weights in each hand called halteres. By swinging your arms forward you gain extra momentum.

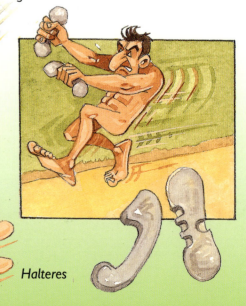

DEADLY DISCUS

There are several Greek myths involving sporting competitions. In one, a king is killed when his son accidentally hits him on the head with a discus. Aim carefully!

Halteres

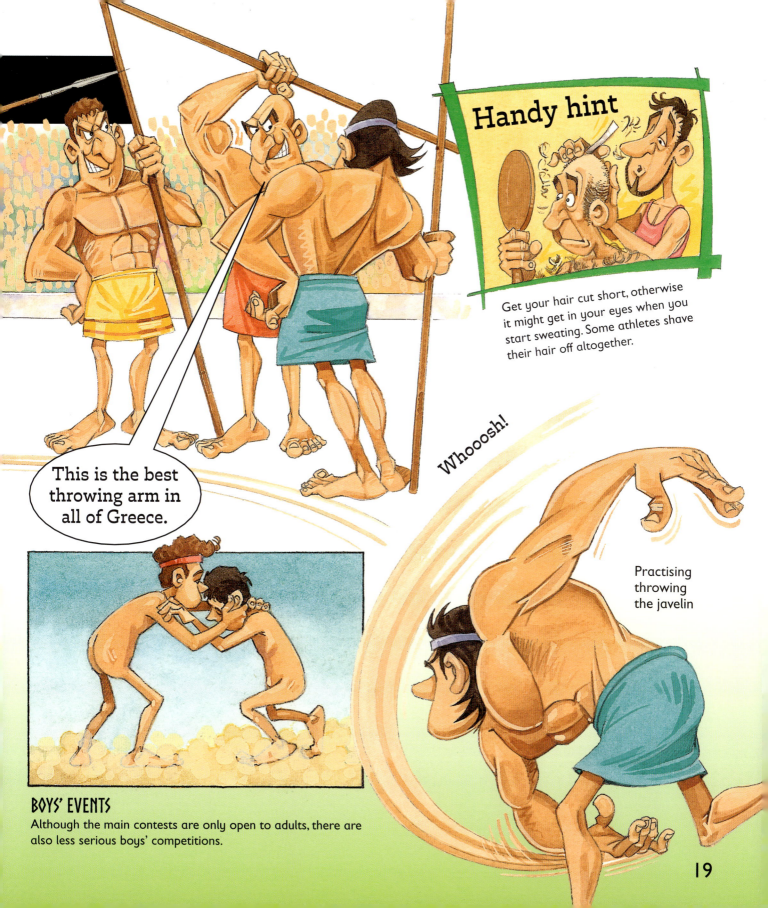

Get your hair cut short, otherwise it might get in your eyes when you start sweating. Some athletes shave their hair off altogether.

This is the best throwing arm in all of Greece.

Whooosh!

Practising throwing the javelin

BOYS' EVENTS

Although the main contests are only open to adults, there are also less serious boys' competitions.

Wrestling

The final event in the pentathlon is wrestling. You are dreading it – competitors are often unable to continue with any other event afterwards because they are so badly injured. The aim of the contest is to trip your opponent and pin him to the floor. He'll be covered in oil and may slip out of your grasp, but by the end you will both be covered in sand anyway. The contest works in heats. Wrestlers are separated into two groups. Pairs then face each other and the winner stays on to fight the winner from another pairing. In this way, there is only one victorious wrestler left at the end. Some wrestlers have been champions for several Games in a row.

RULES

There are guidelines to the competition and tactics such as eye-gouging and biting are forbidden. Unfortunately, it is hard for the referee to see everything that goes on, so everyone bends the rules.

BOXERS

Boxers also take part in the Games. They are terrifying to look at. They wear leather padding on their hands, some with metal studs to inflict extra pain on their opponents.

PANCRATIUM

Just about anything goes in this event. It is a mixture of boxing and wrestling. Competitors are allowed to choke and punch each other, even when they are on the floor. Fighters have been known to die from their injuries.

WEIGHT CLASSES

No allowance is made for differences in size of opponents. You might well end up fighting someone who is twice as big as you!

Handy hint

Face your opponent with the sun behind you. The light will dazzle him and might give you an advantage.

REFEREES

Referees observe all the events and try to steer clear of any flying limbs. If they catch any rule-breakers, they will tap the offender with their stick.

Do you give up yet?

Referee

21

On horseback

Some of the most popular events at the Olympics happen at the hippodrome. This contains a 200m-long horse track with a turning post at each end. In one event, jockeys race on horseback without saddles. It's not a comfortable ride! Chariot races are also popular. Like many aspects of the Games, this is seen as good practice for war, where warriors drive chariots into battle.

Up to 40 chariots take part in a single race, so the sport is very dangerous. At the turning posts, all the chariots become tangled up. Collisions are common and accidents and injuries range from minor sprains to broken bones and even death.

JOCKEYS

In horse races, it is the owner of the horse who officially enters the event rather than the rider. This means that owners can select young boys (lighter than fully-grown men) as jockeys for their horses.

KEEPING UP

One type of race involves riders jumping off their horses and running by their side.

Aaargh! Someone loosened my chariot's bolts!

Handy hint

It is much better to own a race horse than to ride it. As well as being safe from injury, it is the owner who receives a prize, not the rider.

'FIXING' CHARIOTS

Check your chariot before racing. Another competitor might have loosened a bolt or two, to make you crash during the race.

23

Rivalries

War has recently broken out between the city-states of Sparta and Athens. During the Persian Wars, Spartans and Athenians fought together to defend Greece, but the two could not be more different. Athens is a centre of culture and learning, whereas Sparta is a military state where the majority of people are slaves and all the male citizens are soldiers. They have a fearsome reputation. During the Games, states are supposed to suspend their conflicts, but in reality this is impossible. Although no one is allowed to bring weapons into the Games, regional pride fuels the competition and brawls often break out between traditional rivals.

I've seen Spartan women — I bet your wife is hairier than you!

SEARCHED

On their way into the Games, spectators and athletes alike are searched for weapons. It is an offence to the gods to bring violence into the sacred area of Olympia.

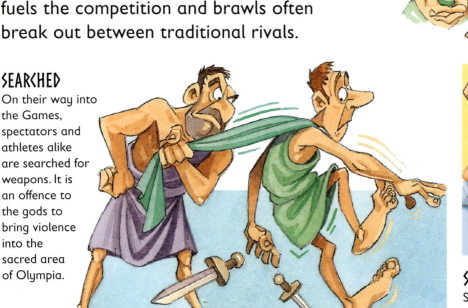

SPARTAN CHILDREN

Spartan children are not treated well. Their harsh childhood prepares them for later life and military service.

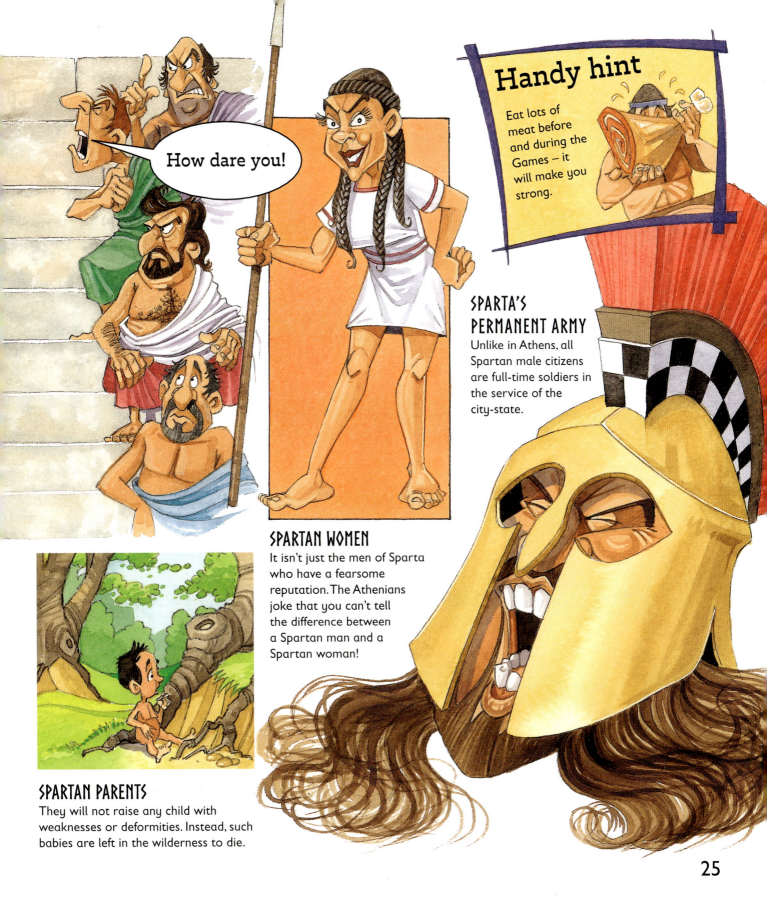

How dare you!

Handy hint

Eat lots of meat before and during the Games – it will make you strong.

SPARTA'S PERMANENT ARMY

Unlike in Athens, all Spartan male citizens are full-time soldiers in the service of the city-state.

SPARTAN WOMEN

It isn't just the men of Sparta who have a fearsome reputation. The Athenians joke that you can't tell the difference between a Spartan man and a Spartan woman!

SPARTAN PARENTS

They will not raise any child with weaknesses or deformities. Instead, such babies are left in the wilderness to die.

25

Obeying the rules

Every contest is watched closely by referees to make sure that no one is cheating. Tactics such as tripping other runners, or trying to distract a javelin thrower, are frowned upon. Cheaters may be disqualified or forced to pay a fine to the Olympic committee. Since you have no money, your father or village will have to pay for you. The worst crime of all is bribing a referee or opponent, as this is completely against the spirit of the Games. It is also forbidden to kill your opponent in the wrestling and boxing matches, either deliberately or accidentally.

BRIBING A REFEREE
The Greeks take the Games very seriously. The worst possible crime you can commit is to give a referee money in return for favours.

FLOGGING
As well as fines and disqualification, competitors can be whipped with a stick if they break the rules.

Referee

THE FINAL WORD
The referees are in charge at the Games. You cannot appeal against their decisions.

Referee

PAYMENT TO THE GODS
If you do break the rules, you might be made to pay a fine. All around the sanctuary are shrines which have been constructed with penalty money.

Shrine to Zeus

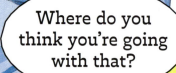

Where do you think you're going with that?

Victory or defeat?

After all the pain and hard work, you triumph in the pentathlon. For the winners, the prizes are small. Although it is forbidden, money can be made by gambling on the outcome of the events. For most competitors though, the reputation gained through victory is reward enough. The losers get nothing but disappointment or shame, and some even lose their lives in the contest. As the crowds leave Olympia, many people will find themselves at war once again. You may have to join the army and fight against the Spartans. If you survive, will you be back to compete in the Games in four years' time?

Congratulations on your victory.

Laurel wreath

Jar of olive oil

PRIZES

There are no medals or large amounts of cash for winning at the Olympics. Prizes are simply a wreath of laurel leaves to wear on your head, or a decorated jar of olive oil. And, of course, pride in your achievement.

Statue of a victorious athlete

Poet

Handy hint

Have a son. Soon it will be his turn to represent the family.

FAME, BUT NO FORTUNE

The Greeks are artistic people, brimming with creativity and a deep appreciation for beauty. If you are lucky, a famous craftsman might choose you as a subject, immortalising your figure and achievements in stone for all to admire, or perhaps a poet will celebrate your victories and noble acts in verse, to be recited in the vibrant halls and amphitheaters.

HOMECOMING

When you arrive back in Athens, you are a minor celebrity. People from miles around gather to celebrate your return. But soon it will be life as normal – back to work on the farm.

29

Glossary

Acropolis The name of the hill in Athens which housed the main official buildings of the city-state, including the Parthenon.

Aidos The Greek oath of sportsmanship, sworn by an athlete taking part in the Olympic Games.

Athlete A term from the Greek meaning 'one who competes'.

Chariot A horse-drawn vehicle used by Greek soldiers in battle.

City-state A small, independent kingdom in ancient Greece.

Compulsory Something that you have no choice but to do or perform.

Democracy A society where all citizens can have a say, or vote, in the way that the society operates.

Discus A disk thrown by athletes.

Disqualification When a person is not allowed to take any further part in a competition because they have broken the rules.

Ephebe The name given to an Athenian male at the age of **18** who is about to undertake military service.

Flautist A person who plays the flute.

Halteres Clay or metal weights carried by a long-jumper to give him extra momentum through the air.

Hippodrome The track where horse racing took place. From the Greek, *hippos* (horse) and *dromos* (racecourse).

Olympiad The period, every four years, when the Olympic Games take place.

Palaestra A sports or exercise ground in Ancient Greece.

Pancratium A brutal sport which was a mixture of boxing and wrestling, with few rules to prevent serious injury.

Parthenon The temple of the goddess Athena which stood on the Acropolis in Athens.

Persia The huge empire which covered much of the area east of Greece, c. 550–350 BC.

Pilgrim A person who undertakes a religious journey.

Sanctuary A sacred or holy place where ancient Greeks worshipped a god or goddess.

Sparta The second most prominent city-state in fifth-century BC Greece, famed for its emphasis on a strict military life.

Stadium A running track.

Stylus A pointed stick used for inscribing letters on a wax tablet.

Truce An agreement to suspend fighting a war.

Wreath A band or ring of intertwined leaves or flowers.

31

Index